FEB 2 7 2018

YOU CAN CONTROL YOUR VOICE LOUD OR QUIET?

You Choose the Ending

by Connie Colwell Miller • illustrated by Victoria Assanelli

Do you ever wish you could change a story or choose a different ending?

IN THESE BOOKS, YOU CAN!

Read along and when you see this:

WHAT HAPPENS NEXT?

Skip to the page for that choice, and see what happens.

In this story, Haneen is excited at the library. Will she be loud or quiet? Help Haneen make choices about her voice by reading this book.

Haneen's mom is taking her to the library. Haneen loves the library. She bursts through the front door and sees an exciting book.

WHAT HAPPENS NEXT?

→ If Haneen calls loudly to her mother, turn the page.

If Haneen whispers, turn to page 20. ←

"Mom!" Haneen shouts. "Look at this new book about fairies!"

Mom frowns. "I'm happy you found a book, Haneen," her mother says, "but in the library you need to use a quiet voice. Try again."

WHAT HAPPENS NEXT?

If Haneen uses her loud voice again, turn the page.
If she brings her voice down, turn to page 18.

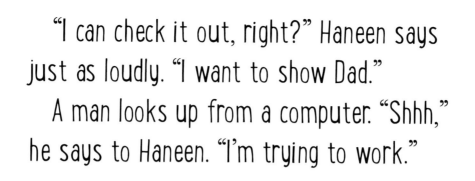

"I can check it out, right?" Haneen says just as loudly. "I want to show Dad."

A man looks up from a computer. "Shhh," he says to Haneen. "I'm trying to work."

6

WHAT HAPPENS NEXT?

If Haneen ignores the man, turn the page.
If she says she's sorry, turn to page 14.

Then Haneen sees her friend Amy from school. She forgets her voice again. "Amy!" Haneen shouts. "Amy! Hello!"

TURN THE PAGE →

"Haneen!" her mother scolds. "Stop and listen. What do you hear?"

Haneen stops. She listens.

"I hear typing," Haneen says. "I hear a pencil on paper. That's all."

TURN THE PAGE →

"You can use a loud voice sometimes, but not in here," Haneen's mother says. "Since you can't control your voice, we'll have to go home."

Haneen doesn't get to check out a book or talk to Amy. She will use a quiet voice the next time she comes to the library.

THE END

Go to page 23.

Haneen stops. She looks at the man's face. She sees he is upset.
"I'm sorry," Haneen says to the man. "I was too loud."

TURN THE PAGE ⟶

"Thank you for apologizing, Haneen," her mother says, "but I think we should check out the book and go home."

Haneen is disappointed that she can't stay longer, but she knows she should have used a quiet voice in the library.

THE END

→ Go to page 23. ←

Haneen stops and looks around. Some people are reading books. Others are working on computers. All the people look like they are thinking. Haneen thinks about how these are quiet tasks.

TURN THE PAGE →

Before she speaks, Haneen listens carefully. She
matches her voice to the quiet sounds she hears.

"Mom," she says softly, "Look at this amazing book!"

TURN THE PAGE →

Because she was quiet in the library, she gets to spend time there with her mom. She checks out two books. Haneen is proud of herself for controlling her voice.

THE END

- What choices did you pick for Haneen? How did that story end?
- What helped Haneen to understand she needed to use a quieter voice? Do you need reminders, too?
- Where should you use a quiet voice? Where is it okay to be loud?

We are all free to make choices, but choices have consequences. What would YOU do if you were very excited and couldn't control your voice?

For Haneen and the new baby, with love. —C.C.M.

AMICUS ILLUSTRATED and AMICUS INK
are published by Amicus
P.O. Box 1329, Mankato, MN 56002
www.amicuspublishing.us

Library of Congress Cataloging-in-Publication Data
Names: Miller, Connie Colwell, 1976- author. | Assanelli, Victoria, 1984- illustrator.
Title: You can control your voice : loud or quiet? / by Connie Colwell Miller ;
    illustrated by Victoria Assanelli.
Description: Mankato, Minnesota : Amicus Illustrated, [2018] | Series: Making
    good choices | Audience: K to grade 3.
Identifiers: LCCN 2016057209 (print) | LCCN 2017011716 (ebook) |
    ISBN 9781681512570 (pdf) | ISBN 9781681511672 (library binding) |
    ISBN 9781681522364 (pbk.)
Subjects: LCSH: Library etiquette—Juvenile literature. | Decision making in
    children—Juvenile literature.
Classification: LCC Z716.43 (ebook) | LCC Z716.43 .M55 2018 (print) | DDC
    395.5/3—dc23
LC record available at https://lccn.loc.gov/2016057209

Editor: Rebecca Glaser
Designer: Kathleen Petelinsek

Printed in North Mankato, Minnesota
HC   10 9 8 7 6 5 4 3
PB   10 9 8 7 6 5 4 3 2 1

ABOUT THE AUTHOR

Connie Colwell Miller is a writer, editor, and instructor who lives in Mankato, Minnesota, with her four children. She has written over 80 books for young children. She likes to tell stories to her kids to teach them important life lessons.

ABOUT THE ILLUSTRATOR

Victoria Assanelli was born during the autumn of 1984 in Buenos Aires, Argentina. She spent most of her childhood playing with her grandparents, reading books, and drawing doodles. She began working as an illustrator in 2007, and has illustrated several textbooks and storybooks since.